The original "Steele Dossier," in its entirety, as composed by Christopher Steele who used to work for British Intelligence, until retirement in 2009 around which time he founded the company Fusion GPS.

In October 2015, private investigative firm Fusion GPS was contracted by The Washington Free Beacon to provide political opposition research against Trump. In April 2016, attorney Marc Elias separately hired Fusion GPS to investigate Trump on behalf of Hillary Clinton's campaign and the DNC.

This is basic Intelligence tradecraft which falls under the heading of propaganda. It is now generally known that Hillary Clinton paid a private firm to construct a document to 'slip' to the FBI to attempt to use the document against her political rival, Donald Trump.

In June 2016, Fusion GPS subcontracted Steele's firm to compile the dossier and investigate Donald Trump with the hopes of damaging Trump's campaign. The FBI apparently did little to no investigation into the source of the document in the early stages.

Following Trump's election as president, funding from Clinton and the DNC ceased, but Steele continued his research and was reportedly paid directly by Fusion GPS co-founder Glenn R. Simpson. The completed dossier was then handed to British and American intelligence services.

On Fox News and in the National Review, McCarthy makes three primary arguments: (1) the so-called Steele dossier was "the driving force behind the Trump-Russia investigation"; (2) the FISA court was not told that the Clinton campaign was behind Steele's work; and (3) the FBI did not "verify" the factual allegations contained in the dossier.

The Clinton campaign paid Perkins Coie $5.6 million in legal fees from June 2015 to December 2016, according to campaign finance records, and the DNC paid the firm $3.6 million in "legal and compliance consulting" since November 2015 — though it's impossible to tell from the filings how much of that work was for other legal matters and how much of it related to Fusion GPS.

The following is the unedited " Steele Dossier "

COMPANY INTELLIGENCE REPORT 2016/080

US PRESIDENTIAL ELECTION: REPUBLICAN CANDIDATE DONALD TRUMP'S ACTIVITIES IN RUSSIA AND COMPROMISING RELATIONSHIP WITH THE KREMLIN

Summary

- Russian regime has been cultivating, supporting and assisting TRUMP for at least 5 years. Aim, endorsed by PUTIN, has been to encourage splits and divisions in western alliance

- So far TRUMP has declined various sweetener real estate business deals offered him in Russia in order to further the Kremlin's cultivation of him. However he and his inner circle have accepted a regular flow of intelligence from the Kremlin, including on his Democratic and other political rivals

- Former top Russian intelligence officer claims FSB has compromised TRUMP through his activities in Moscow sufficiently to be able to blackmail him. According to several knowledgeable sources, his conduct in Moscow has included perverted sexual acts which have been arranged/monitored by the FSB

- A dossier of compromising material on Hillary CLINTON has been collated by the Russian Intelligence Services over many years and mainly comprises bugged conversations she had on various visits to Russia and intercepted phone calls rather than any embarrassing conduct. The dossier is controlled by Kremlin spokesman, PESKOV, directly on PUTIN's orders. However it has not as yet been distributed abroad, including to TRUMP. Russian intentions for its deployment still unclear

Detail

1. Speaking to a trusted compatriot in June 2016 sources A and B, a senior Russian Foreign Ministry figure and a former top level Russian intelligence officer still active inside the Kremlin respectively, the Russian authorities had been cultivating and supporting US Republican presidential candidate, Donald TRUMP for at least 5 years. Source B asserted that the TRUMP operation was both supported and directed by Russian President Vladimir PUTIN. Its aim was to sow discord and

disunity both within the US itself, but more especially within the Transatlantic alliance which was viewed as inimical to Russia's interests. Source C, a senior Russian financial official said the TRUMP operation should be seen in terms of PUTIN's desire to return to Nineteenth Century 'Great Power' politics anchored upon countries' interests rather than the ideals-based international order established after World War Two. S/he had overheard PUTIN talking in this way to close associates on several occasions.

2. In terms of specifics, Source A confided that the Kremlin had been feeding TRUMP and his team valuable intelligence on his opponents, including Democratic presidential candidate Hillary CLINTON, for several years (see more below). This was confirmed by Source D, a close associate of TRUMP who had organized and managed his recent trips to Moscow, and who reported, also in June 2016, that this Russian intelligence had been "very helpful". The Kremlin's cultivation operation on TRUMP also had comprised offering him various lucrative real estate development business deals in Russia, especially in relation to the ongoing 2018 World Cup soccer tournament. However, so far, for reasons unknown, TRUMP had not taken up any of these.

3. However, there were other aspects to TRUMP's engagement with the Russian authorities. One which had borne fruit for them was to exploit TRUMP's personal obsessions and sexual perversion in order to obtain suitable 'kompromat' (compromising material) on him. According to Source D, where s/he had been present, TRUMP's (perverted) conduct in Moscow included hiring the presidential suite of the Ritz Carlton Hotel, where he knew President and Mrs OBAMA (whom he hated) had stayed on one of their official trips to Russia, and defiling the bed where they had slept by employing a number of prostitutes to perform a 'golden showers' (urination) show in front of him. The hotel was known to be under FSB control with microphones and concealed cameras in all the main rooms to record anything they wanted to.

4. The Moscow Ritz Carlton episode involving TRUMP reported above was confirmed by Source E, ████████████████████████████████████ who said that s/he and several of the staff were aware of it at the time and subsequently. S/he believed it had happened in 2013. Source E provided an introduction for a company ethnic Russian operative to Source F, a female staffer at the hotel when TRUMP had stayed there, who also confirmed the story. Speaking separately in June 2016, Source B (the former top level Russian intelligence officer) asserted that TRUMP's unorthodox behavior in Russia over the years had provided the authorities there with enough embarrassing material on the now Republican presidential candidate to be able to blackmail him if they so wished.

5. Asked about the Kremlin's reported intelligence feed to TRUMP over recent years and rumours about a Russian dossier of 'kompromat' on

Hillary CLINTON (being circulated), Source B confirmed the file's existence. S/he confided in a trusted compatriot that it had been collated by Department K of the FSB for many years, dating back to her husband Bill's presidency, and comprised mainly eavesdropped conversations of various sorts rather than details/evidence of unorthodox or embarrassing behavior. Some of the conversations were from bugged comments CLINTON had made on her various trips to Russia and focused on things she had said which contradicted her current position on various issues. Others were most probably from phone intercepts.

6. Continuing on this theme, Source G, a senior Kremlin official, confided that the CLINTON dossier was controlled exclusively by chief Kremlin spokesman, Dmitriy PESKOV, who was responsible for compiling/handling it on the explicit instructions of PUTIN himself. The dossier however had not as yet been made available abroad, including to TRUMP or his campaign team. At present it was unclear what PUTIN's intentions were in this regard.

20 June 2016

COMPANY INTELLIGENCE REPORT 2016/086

RUSSIA/CYBER CRIME: A SYNOPSIS OF RUSSIAN STATE SPONSORED AND OTHER CYBER OFFENSIVE (CRIMINAL) OPERATIONS

Summary

- Russia has extensive programme of state-sponsored offensive cyber operations. External targets include foreign governments and big corporations, especially banks. FSB leads on cyber within Russian apparatus. Limited success in attacking top foreign targets like G7 governments, security services and IFIs but much more on second tier ones through IT back doors, using corporate and other visitors to Russia

- FSB often uses coercion and blackmail to recruit most capable cyber operatives in Russia into its state-sponsored programmes. Heavy use also, both wittingly and unwittingly, of CIS emigres working in western corporations and ethnic Russians employed by neighbouring governments e.g. Latvia

- Example cited of successful Russian cyber operation targeting senior Western business visitor. Provided back door into important Western institutions.

- Example given of US citizen of Russian origin approached by FSB and offered incentive of "investment" in his business when visiting Moscow.

- Problems however for Russian authorities themselves in countering local hackers and cyber criminals, operating outside state control. Central Bank claims there were over 20 serious attacks on correspondent accounts held by CBR in 2015, comprising Roubles several billion in fraud

- Some details given of leading non-state Russian cyber criminal groups

Details

1. Speaking in June 2016, a number of Russian figures with a detailed knowledge of national cyber crime, both state-sponsored and otherwise, outlined the current situation in this area. A former senior intelligence officer divided Russian state-sponsored offensive cyber operations into four categories (in order of priority):- targeting foreign, especially

western governments; penetrating leading foreign business corporations, especially banks; domestic monitoring of the elite; and attacking political opponents both at home and abroad. The former intelligence officer reported that the Federal Security Service (FSB) was the lead organization within the Russian state apparatus for cyber operations.

2. In terms of the success of Russian offensive cyber operations to date, a senior government figure reported that there had been only limited success in penetrating the "first tier" foreign targets. These comprised western (especially G7 and NATO) governments, security and intelligence services and central banks, and the IFIs. To compensate for this shortfall, massive effort had been invested, with much greater success, in attacking the "secondary targets", particularly western private banks and the governments of smaller states allied to the West. S/he mentioned Latvia in this regard. Hundreds of agents, either consciously cooperating with the FSB or whose personal and professional IT systems had been unwittingly compromised, were recruited. Many were people who had ethnic and family ties to Russia and/or had been incentivized financially to cooperate. Such people often would receive monetary inducements or contractual favours from the Russian state or its agents in return. This had created difficulties for parts of the Russian state apparatus in obliging/indulging them e.g. the Central Bank of Russia knowingly having to cover up for such agents' money laundering operations through the Russian financial system.

3. In terms of the FSB's recruitment of capable cyber operatives to carry out its, ideally deniable, offensive cyber operations, a Russian IT specialist with direct knowledge reported in June 2016 that this was often done using coercion and blackmail. In terms of 'foreign' agents, the FSB was approaching US citizens of Russian (Jewish) origin on business trips to Russia. In one case a US citizen of Russian ethnicity had been visiting Moscow to attract investors in his new information technology program. The FSB clearly knew this and had offered to provide seed capital to this person in return for them being able to access and modify his IP, with a view to targeting priority foreign targets by planting a Trojan virus in the software. The US visitor was told this was common practice. The FSB also had implied significant operational success as a result of installing cheap Russian IT games containing their own malware unwittingly by targets on their PCs and other platforms.

4. In a more advanced and successful FSB operation, an IT operator inside a leading Russian SOE, who previously had been employed on conventional (defensive) IT work there, had been under instruction for the last year to conduct an offensive cyber operation against a foreign director of the company. Although the latter was apparently an infrequent visitor to Russia, the FSB now successfully had penetrated his personal IT and through this had managed to access various important institutions in the West through the back door.

5. In terms of other technical IT platforms, an FSB cyber operative flagged up the 'Telegram' enciphered commercial system as having been of especial concern and therefore heavily targeted by the FSB, not least because it was used frequently by Russian internal political activists and oppositionists. His/her understanding was that the FSB now successfully had cracked this communications software and therefore it was no longer secure to use.

6. The senior Russian government figure cited above also reported that non-state sponsored cyber crime was becoming an increasing problem inside Russia for the government and authorities there. The Central Bank of Russia claimed that in 2015 alone there had been more than 20 attempts at serious cyber embezzlement of money from corresponding accounts held there, comprising several billions Roubles. More generally, s/he understood there were circa 15 major organised crime groups in the country involved in cyber crime, all of which continued to operate largely outside state and FSB control. These included the so-called 'Anunak', 'Buktrap' and 'Metel' organisations.

26 July 2015

COMPANY INTELLIGENCE REPORT 2016/095

RUSSIA/US PRESIDENTIAL ELECTION: FURTHER INDICATIONS OF EXTENSIVE CONSPIRACY BETWEEN TRUMP'S CAMPAIGN TEAM AND THE KREMLIN

Summary

- Further evidence of extensive conspiracy between TRUMP's campaign team and Kremlin, sanctioned at highest levels and involving Russian diplomatic staff based in the US

- TRUMP associate admits Kremlin behind recent appearance of DNC e-mails on WikiLeaks, as means of maintaining plausible deniability

- Agreed exchange of information established in both directions. TRUMP's team using moles within DNC and hackers in the US as well as outside in Russia. PUTIN motivated by fear and hatred of Hillary CLINTON. Russians receiving intel from TRUMP's team on Russian oligarchs and their families in US

- Mechanism for transmitting this intelligence involves "pension" disbursements to Russian emigres living in US as cover, using consular officials in New York, DC and Miami

- Suggestion from source close to TRUMP and MANAFORT that Republican campaign team happy to have Russia as media bogeyman to mask more extensive corrupt business ties to China and other emerging countries

Detail

1. Speaking in confidence to a compatriot in late July 2016, Source E, an ethnic Russian close associate of Republican US presidential candidate Donald TRUMP, admitted that there was a well-developed conspiracy of co-operation between them and the Russian leadership. This was managed on the TRUMP side by the Republican candidate's campaign manager, Paul MANAFORT, who was using foreign policy advisor, Carter PAGE, and others as intermediaries. The two sides had a mutual interest in defeating Democratic presidential candidate Hillary CLINTON, whom President PUTIN apparently both hated and feared.

2. Inter alia, Source E, acknowledged that the Russian regime had been behind the recent leak of embarrassing e-mail messages, emanating from the Democratic National Committee (DNC), to the WikiLeaks platform.

The reason for using WikiLeaks was "plausible deniability" and the operation had been conducted with the full knowledge and support of TRUMP and senior members of his campaign team. In return the TRUMP team had agreed to sideline Russian intervention in Ukraine as a campaign issue and to raise US/NATO defence commitments in the Baltics and Eastern Europe to deflect attention away from Ukraine, a priority for PUTIN who needed to cauterise the subject.

3. In the wider context of TRUMP campaign/Kremlin co-operation, Source E claimed that the intelligence network being used against CLINTON comprised three elements. Firstly there were agents/facilitators within the Democratic Party structure itself, secondly Russian emigre and associated offensive cyber operators based in the US; and thirdly, state-sponsored cyber operatives working in Russia. All three elements had played an important role to date. On the mechanism for rewarding relevant assets based in the US, and effecting a two-way flow of intelligence and other useful information, Source E claimed that Russian diplomatic staff in key cities such as New York, Washington DC and Miami were using the emigre 'pension' distribution system as cover. The operation therefore depended on key people in the US Russian emigre community for its success. Tens of thousands of dollars were involved.

4. In terms of the intelligence flow from the TRUMP team to Russia, Source E reported that much of this concerned the activities of business oligarchs and their families' activities and assets in the US, with which PUTIN and the Kremlin seemed preoccupied.

5. Commenting on the negative media publicity surrounding alleged Russian interference in the US election campaign in support of TRUMP, Source E said he understood that the Republican candidate and his team were relatively relaxed about this because it deflected media and the Democrats' attention away from TRUMP's business dealings in China and other emerging markets. Unlike in Russia, these were substantial and involved the payment of large bribes and kickbacks which, were they to become public, would be potentially very damaging to their campaign.

6. Finally, regarding TRUMP's claimed minimal investment profile in Russia, a separate source with direct knowledge said this had not been for want of trying. TRUMP's previous efforts had included exploring the real estate sector in St Petersburg as well as Moscow but in the end TRUMP had had to settle for the use of extensive sexual services there from local prostitutes rather than business success.

COMPANY INTELLIGENCE REPORT 2016/94

RUSSIA: SECRET KREMLIN MEETINGS ATTENDED BY TRUMP ADVISOR, CARTER PAGE IN MOSCOW (JULY 2016)

Summary

- TRUMP advisor Carter PAGE holds secret meetings in Moscow with SECHIN and senior Kremlin Internal Affairs official, DIVYEKIN

- SECHIN raises issues of future bilateral US-Russia energy co-operation and associated lifting of western sanctions against Russia over Ukraine. PAGE non-committal in response

- DIVEYKIN discusses release of Russian dossier of 'kompromat' on TRUMP's opponent, Hillary CLINTON, but also hints at Kremlin possession of such material on TRUMP

Detail

1. Speaking in July 2016, a Russian source close to Rosneft President, PUTIN close associate and US-sanctioned individual, Igor SECHIN, confided the details of a recent secret meeting between him and visiting Foreign Affairs Advisor to Republican presidential candidate Donald TRUMP, Carter PAGE.

2. According to SECHIN's associate, the Rosneft President (CEO) had raised with PAGE the issues of future bilateral energy cooperation and prospects for an associated move to lift Ukraine-related western sanctions against Russia. PAGE had reacted positively to this demarche by SECHIN but had been generally non-committal in response.

3. Speaking separately, also in July 2016, an official close to Presidential Administration Head, S. IVANOV, confided in a compatriot that a senior colleague in the Internal Political Department of the PA, DIVYEKIN (nfd) also had met secretly with PAGE on his recent visit. Their agenda had included DIVEYKIN raising a dossier of 'kompromat' the Kremlin possessed on TRUMP's Democratic presidential rival, Hillary CLINTON, and its possible release to the Republican's campaign team.

4. However, the Kremlin official close to S. IVANOV added that s/he believed DIVEYKIN also had hinted (or indicated more strongly) that the Russian leadership also had 'kompromat' on TRUMP which the latter should bear in mind in his dealings with them.

19 July 2016

COMPANY INTELLIGENCE REPORT 2016/097

RUSSIA-US PRESIDENTIAL ELECTION: KREMLIN CONCERN THAT POLITICAL FALLOUT FROM DNC E-MAIL HACKING AFFAIR SPIRALLING OUT OF CONTROL

Summary

- Kremlin concerned that political fallout from DNC e-mail hacking operation is spiralling out of control. Extreme nervousness among TRUMP's associates as result of negative media attention/accusations

- Russians meanwhile keen to cool situation and maintain 'plausible deniability' of existing /ongoing pro-TRUMP and anti-CLINTON operations. Therefore unlikely to be any ratcheting up offensive plays in immediate future

- Source close to TRUMP campaign however confirms regular exchange with Kremlin has existed for at least 8 years, including intelligence fed back to Russia on oligarchs' activities in US

- Russians apparently have promised not to use 'kompromat' they hold on TRUMP as leverage, given high levels of voluntary co-operation forthcoming from his team

Detail

1. Speaking in confidence to a trusted associate in late July 2016, a Russian émigré figure close to the Republican US presidential candidate Donald TRUMP's campaign team commented on the fallout from publicity surrounding the Democratic National Committee (DNC) e-mail hacking scandal. The émigré said there was a high level of anxiety within the TRUMP team as a result of various accusations levelled against them and indications from the Kremlin that President PUTIN and others in the leadership thought things had gone too far now and risked spiralling out of control.

2. Continuing on this theme, the émigré associate of TRUMP opined that the Kremlin wanted the situation to calm but for 'plausible deniability' to be maintained concerning its (extensive) pro-TRUMP and anti-CLINTON operations. S/he therefore judged that it was unlikely these would be ratcheted up, at least for the time being.

3. However, in terms of established operational liaison between the TRUMP team and the Kremlin, the émigré confirmed that an intelligence exchange had been running between them for at least 8 years. Within this context PUTIN's priority requirement had been for intelligence on the activities, business and otherwise, in the US of leading Russian oligarchs and their families. TRUMP and his associates duly had obtained and supplied the Kremlin with this information.

4. Finally, the émigré said s/he understood the Kremlin had more intelligence on CLINTON and her campaign but he did not know the details or when or if it would be released. As far as 'kompromat' (compromising information) on TRUMP were concerned, although there was plenty of this, he understood the Kremlin had given its word that it would not be deployed against the Republican presidential candidate given how helpful and co-operative his team had been over several years, and particularly of late.

30 July 2016

12

COMPANY INTELLIGENCE REPORT 2016/100

RUSSIA/USA: GROWING BACKLASH IN KREMLIN TO DNC HACKING AND
TRUMP SUPPORT OPERATIONS

Summary

- Head of PA IVANOV laments Russian intervention in US presidential
  election and black PR against CLINTON and the DNC. Vows not to supply
  intelligence to Kremlin PR operatives again. Advocates now sitting tight
  and denying everything

- Presidential spokesman PESKOV the main protagonist in Kremlin
  campaign to aid TRUMP and damage CLINTON. He is now scared and
  fears being made scapegoat by leadership for backlash in US. Problem
  compounded by his botched intervention in recent Turkish crisis

- Premier MEDVEDEV's office furious over DNC hacking and associated
  anti-Russian publicity. Want good relations with US and ability to travel
  there. Refusing to support or help cover up after PESKOV

- Talk now in Kremlin of TRUMP withdrawing from presidential race
  altogether, but this still largely wishful thinking by more liberal elements
  in Moscow

Detail

1. Speaking in early August 2016, two well-placed and established Kremlin
   sources outlined the divisions and backlash in Moscow arising from the
   leaking of Democratic National Committee (DNC) e-mails and the wider
   pro-TRUMP operation being conducted in the US. Head of Presidential
   Administration, Sergei IVANOV, was angry at the recent turn of events.
   He believed the Kremlin "team" involved, led by presidential spokesman
   Dmitriy PESKOV, had gone too far in interfering in foreign affairs with
   their "elephant in a china shop black PR". IVANOV claimed always to have
   opposed the handling and exploitation of intelligence by this PR "team".
   Following the backlash against such foreign interference in US politics,
   IVANOV was advocating that the only sensible course of action now for
   the Russian leadership was to "sit tight and deny everything".

2. Continuing on this theme the source close to IVANOV reported that
   PESKOV now was "scared shitless" that he would be scapegoated by
   PUTIN and the Kremlin and held responsible for the backlash against
   Russian political interference in the US election. IVANOV was determined

to stop PESKOV playing an independent role in relation to the US going forward and the source fully expected the presidential spokesman now to lay low. PESKOV's position was not helped by a botched attempt by him also to interfere in the recent failed coup in Turkey from a government relations (GR) perspective (no further details).

3. The extent of disquiet and division within Moscow caused by the backlash against Russian interference in the US election was underlined by a second source, close to premier Dmitriy MEDVEDEV (DAM). S/he said the Russian prime minister and his colleagues wanted to have good relations with the US, regardless of who was in power there, and not least so as to be able to travel there in future, either officially or privately. They were openly refusing to cover up for PESKOV and others involved in the DNC/TRUMP operations or to support his counter-attack of allegations against the USG for its alleged hacking of the Russian government and state agencies.

4. According to the first source, close to IVANOV, there had been talk in the Kremlin of TRUMP being forced to withdraw from the presidential race altogether as a result of recent events, ostensibly on grounds of his psychological state and unsuitability for high office. This might not be so bad for Russia in the circumstances but in the view of the source, it remained largely wishful thinking on the part of those in the regime opposed to PESKOV and his "botched" operations, at least for the time being.

5 August 2016

RUSSIA/US PRESIDENTIAL ELECTION: SENIOR KREMLIN FIGURE OUTLINES EVOLVING RUSSIAN TACTICS IN PRO-TRUMP, ANTI-CLINTON OPERATION

Summary

- Head of PA, IVANOV assesses Kremlin intervention in US presidential election and outlines leadership thinking on operational way forward

- No new leaks envisaged, as too politically risky, but rather further exploitation of (WikiLeaks) material already disseminated to exacerbate divisions

- Educated US youth to be targeted as protest (against CLINTON) and swing vote in attempt to turn them over to TRUMP

- Russian leadership, including PUTIN, celebrating perceived success to date in splitting US hawks and elite

- Kremlin engaging with several high profile US players, including STEIN, PAGE and (former DIA Director Michael Flynn), and funding their recent visits to Moscow

Details

1. Speaking in confidence to a close colleague in early August 2016, Head of the Russian Presidential Administration (PA), Sergei IVANOV, assessed the impact and results of Kremlin intervention in the US presidential election to date. Although most commentators believed that the Kremlin was behind the leaked DNC/CLINTON e-mails, this remained technically deniable. Therefore the Russians would not risk their position for the time being with new leaked material, even to a third party like WikiLeaks. Rather the tactics would be to spread rumours and misinformation about the content of what already had been leaked and make up new content.

2. Continuing on this theme, IVANOV said that the audience to be targeted by such operations was the educated youth in America as the PA assessed that there was still a chance they could be persuaded to vote for Republican candidate Donald TRUMP as a protest against the Washington establishment (in the form of Democratic candidate Hillary CLINTON). The hope was that even if she won, as a result of this CLINTON in power would be bogged down in working for internal reconciliation in the US, rather than being able to focus on foreign policy which would damage Russia's interests. This also should give President PUTIN more room for manoeuvre in the run-up to Russia's own presidential election in 2018.

3. IVANOV reported that although the Kremlin had underestimated the strength of US media and liberal reaction to the DNC hack and TRUMP's links to Russia, PUTIN was generally satisfied with the progress of the anti-CLINTON operation to date. He recently had had a drink with PUTIN to mark this. In IVANOV's view, the US had tried to divide the Russian elite with sanctions but failed, whilst they, by contrast, had succeeded in splitting the US hawks inimical to Russia and the Washington elite more generally, half of whom had refused to endorse any presidential candidate as a result of Russian intervention.

4. Speaking separately, also in early August 2016, a Kremlin official involved in US relations commented on aspects of the Russian operation to date. Its goals had been threefold- asking sympathetic US actors how Moscow could help them; gathering relevant intelligence; and creating and disseminating compromising information ('kompromat'). This had involved the Kremlin supporting various US political figures, including funding indirectly their recent visits to Moscow. S/he named a delegation from Lyndon LAROUCHE; presidential candidate Jill STEIN of the Green Party; TRUMP foreign policy adviser

Carter PAGE; and former DIA Director Michael Flynn, in this regard and as successful in terms of perceived outcomes.

10 August 2016

COMPANY INTELLIGENCE REPORT 2016/102

RUSSIA/US PRESIDENTIAL ELECTION: REACTION IN TRUMP CAMP TO RECENT NEGATIVE PUBLICITY ABOUT RUSSIAN INTERFERENCE AND LIKELY RESULTING TACTICS GOING FORWARD

Summary

- TRUMP campaign insider reports recent DNC e-mail leaks were aimed at switching SANDERS (protest) voters away from CLINTON and over to TRUMP

- Admits Republican campaign underestimated resulting negative reaction from US liberals, elite and media and forced to change course as result

- Need now to turn tables on CLINTON's use of PUTIN as bogeyman in election, although some resentment at Russian president's perceived attempt to undermine USG and system over and above swinging presidential election

Detail

1. Speaking in confidence on 9 August 2016, an ethnic Russian associate of Republican US presidential candidate Donald TRUMP discussed the reaction inside his camp, and revised tactics therein resulting from recent negative publicity concerning Moscow's clandestine involvement in the campaign. TRUMP's associate reported that the aim of leaking the DNC e-mails to WikiLeaks during the Democratic Convention had been to swing supporters of Bernie SANDERS away from Hillary CLINTON and across to TRUMP. These voters were perceived as activist and anti-status quo and anti-establishment and in that regard sharing many features with the TRUMP campaign, including a visceral dislike of Hillary CLINTON. This objective had been conceived and promoted, inter alia, by TRUMP's foreign policy adviser Carter PAGE who had discussed it directly with the ethnic Russian associate.

2. Continuing on this theme, the ethnic Russian associate of TRUMP assessed that the problem was that the TRUMP campaign had underestimated the strength of the negative reaction from liberals and especially the conservative elite to Russian interference. This was forcing a rethink and a likely change of tactics. The main objective in the short term was to check Democratic candidate Hillary CLINTON's successful exploitation of the PUTIN as bogeyman/Russian interference story to tarnish TRUMP and bolster her own (patriotic) credentials. The TRUMP campaign was focusing on tapping into support in the American television media to achieve this, as they reckoned this resource had been underused by them to date.

3. However, TRUMP's associate also admitted that there was a fair amount of anger and resentment within the Republican candidate's team at what was perceived by PUTIN as going beyond the objective of weakening CLINTON and bolstering TRUMP, by attempting to exploit the situation to undermine the US government and democratic system more generally. It was unclear at present how this aspect of the situation would play out in the weeks to come.

10 August 2016

RUSSIA/US PRESIDENTIAL ELECTION: FURTHER DETAILS OF TRUMP LAWYER COHEN'S SECRET LIAISON WITH THE KREMLIN

Summary

- Kremlin insider reports TRUMP lawyer COHEN's secret meeting/s with Kremlin officials in August 2016 was/were held in Prague

- Russian parastatal organisation Rossotrudnichestvo used as cover for this liaison and premises in Czech capital may have been used for the meeting/s

- Pro-PUTIN leading Duma figure, KOSACHEV, reportedly involved as "plausibly deniable" facilitator and may have participated in the August meeting/s with COHEN

Detail

1. Speaking to a compatriot and friend on 19 October 2016, a Kremlin insider provided further details of reported clandestine meeting/s between Republican presidential candidate, Donald TRUMP's lawyer Michael COHEN and Kremlin representatives in August 2016. Although the communication between them had to be cryptic for security reasons, the Kremlin insider clearly indicated to his/her friend that the reported contact/s took place in Prague, Czech Republic.

2. Continuing on this theme, the Kremlin insider highlighted the importance of the Russian parastatal organisation, Rossotrudnichestvo, in this contact between TRUMP campaign representative/s and Kremlin officials. Rossotrudnichestvo was being used as cover for this relationship and its office in Prague may well have been used to host the COHEN/Russian Presidential Administration (PA) meeting/s. It was considered a "plausibly deniable" vehicle for this, whilst remaining entirely under Kremlin control.

3. The Kremlin insider went on to identify leading pro-PUTIN Duma figure, Konstantin KOSACHEV (Head of the Foreign Relations Committee) as an important figure in the TRUMP campaign-Kremlin liaison operation. KOSACHEV, also "plausibly deniable" being part of the Russian legislature rather than executive, had facilitated the contact in Prague and by implication, may have attended the meeting/s with COHEN there in August.

Company Comment

We reported previously, in our Company Intelligence Report 2016/135 of 19 October 2016 from the same source, that COHEN met officials from the PA Legal Department clandestinely in an EU country in August 2016. This was in order to clean up the mess left behind by western media revelations of TRUMP ex-campaign manager MANAFORT's corrupt relationship with the former pro-Russian YANUKOVYCH regime in Ukraine and TRUMP foreign policy advisor, Carter PAGE's secret meetings in Moscow with senior regime figures in July 2016. According to the Kremlin advisor, these meeting/s were originally scheduled for COHEN in Moscow but shifted to what was considered an operationally "soft" EU country when it was judged too compromising for him to travel to the Russian capital.

20 October 2016

COMPANY INTELLIGENCE REPORT 2016/105

RUSSIA/UKRAINE: THE DEMISE OF TRUMP'S CAMPAIGN MANAGER PAUL MANAFORT

Summary

- Ex-Ukrainian President YANUKOVYCH confides directly to PUTIN that he authorised kick-back payments to MANAFORT, as alleged in western media. Assures Russian President however there is no documentary evidence/trail

- PUTIN and Russian leadership remain worried however and sceptical that YANUKOVYCH has fully covered the traces of these payments to TRUMP's former campaign manager

- Close associate of TRUMP explains reasoning behind MANAFORT's recent resignation. Ukraine revelations played part but others wanted MANAFORT out for various reasons, especially LEWANDOWSKI who remains influential

Detail

1. Speaking in late August 2016, in the immediate aftermath of Paul MANAFORT's resignation as campaign manager for US Republican presidential candidate Donald TRUMP, a well-placed Russian figure reported on a recent meeting between President PUTIN and ex-President YANUKOVYCH of Ukraine. This had been held in secret on 15 August near Volgograd, Russia and the western media revelations about MANAFORT and Ukraine had featured prominently on the agenda. YANUKOVYCH had confided in PUTIN that he did authorise and order substantial kick-back payments to MANAFORT as alleged but sought to reassure him that there was no documentary trail left behind which could provide clear evidence of this.

2. Given YANUKOVYCH's (unimpressive) record in covering up his own corrupt tracks in the past, PUTIN and others in the Russian leadership were sceptical about the ex-Ukrainian president's reassurances on this as relating to MANAFORT. They therefore still feared the scandal had legs, especially as MANAFORT had been commercially active in Ukraine right up to the time (in March 2016) when he joined TRUMP's campaign team. For them it therefore remained a point of potential political vulnerability and embarrassment.

3. Speaking separately, also in late August 2016, an American political figure associated with Donald TRUMP and his campaign outlined the reasons behind MANAFORT's recent demise. S/he said it was true that the Ukraine corruption revelations had played a part in this but also, several senior players close to TRUMP had wanted MANAFORT out, primarily to loosen his control on strategy and policy formulation. Of particular importance in this regard was MANAFORT's predecessor as campaign manager, Corey LEWANDOWSKI, who hated MANAFORT personally and remained close to TRUMP with whom he discussed the presidential campaign on a regular basis.

22 August 2016

COMPANY INTELLIGENCE REPORT 2016/111

RUSSIA/US: KREMLIN FALLOUT FROM MEDIA EXPOSURE OF MOSCOW'S INTERFERENCE IN THE US PRESIDENTIAL CAMPAIGN

Summary

- Kremlin orders senior staff to remain silent in media and private on allegations of Russian interference in US presidential campaign

- Senior figure however confirms gist of allegations and reports IVANOV sacked as Head of Administration on account of giving PUTIN poor advice on issue. VAINO selected as his replacement partly because he was not involved in pro-TRUMP, anti-CLINTON operation/s

- Russians do have further 'kompromat' on CLINTON (e-mails) and considering disseminating it after Duma (legislative elections) in late September. Presidential spokesman PESKOV continues to lead on this

- However, equally important is Kremlin objective to shift policy consensus favourably to Russia in US post-OBAMA whoever wins. Both presidential candidates' opposition to TPP and TTIP viewed as a result in this respect

- Senior Russian diplomat withdrawn from Washington embassy on account of potential exposure in US presidential election operation/s

Detail

1. Speaking in confidence to a trusted compatriot in mid-September 2016, a senior member of the Russian Presidential Administration (PA) commented on the political fallout from recent western media revelations about Moscow's intervention, in favour of Donald TRUMP and against Hillary CLINTON, in the US presidential election. The PA official reported that the issue had become incredibly sensitive and that President PUTIN had issued direct orders that Kremlin and government insiders should not discuss it in public or even in private.

2. Despite this, the PA official confirmed, from direct knowledge, that the gist of the allegations was true. PUTIN had been receiving conflicting advice on interfering from three separate and expert groups. On one side had been the Russian ambassador to the US, Sergei KISLYAK, and the Ministry of Foreign Affairs, together with an independent and informal network run by presidential foreign policy advisor, Yuri USHAKOV

(KISLYAK's predecessor in Washington) who had urged caution and the potential negative impact on Russia from the operation/s. On the other side was former PA Head, Sergei IVANOV, backed by Russian Foreign Intelligence (SVR), who had advised PUTIN that the pro-TRUMP, anti-CLINTON operation/s would be both effective and plausibly deniable with little blowback. The first group/s had been proven right and this had been the catalyst in PUTIN's decision to sack IVANOV (unexpectedly) as PA Head in August. His successor, Anton VAINO, had been selected for the job partly because he had not been involved in the US presidential election operation/s.

3. Continuing on this theme, the senior PA official said the situation now was that the Kremlin had further 'kompromat' on candidate CLINTON and had been considering releasing this via "plausibly deniable" channels after the Duma (legislative) elections were out of the way in mid-September. There was however a growing train of thought and associated lobby, arguing that the Russians could still make candidate CLINTON look "weak and stupid" by provoking her into railing against PUTIN and Russia without the need to release more of her e-mails. Presidential Spokesman, Dmitriy PESKOV remained a key figure in the operation, although any final decision on dissemination of further material would be taken by PUTIN himself.

4. The senior PA official also reported that a growing element in Moscow's intervention in the US presidential election campaign was the objective of shifting the US political consensus in Russia's perceived interests regardless of who won. It basically comprised of pushing candidate CLINTON away from President OBAMA's policies. The best example of this was that both candidates now openly opposed the draft trade agreements, TPP and TTIP, which were assessed by Moscow as detrimental to Russian interests. Other issues where the Kremlin was looking to shift the US policy consensus were Ukraine and Syria. Overall however, the presidential election was considered still to be too close to call.

5. Finally, speaking separately to the same compatriot, a senior Russian MFA official reported that as a prophylactic measure, a leading Russian diplomat, Mikhail KULAGIN, had been withdrawn from Washington at short notice because Moscow feared his heavy involvement in the US presidential election operation, including the so-called veterans' pensions ruse (reported previously), would be exposed in the media there. His replacement, Andrei BONDAREV however was clean in this regard.

Company Comment

The substance of what was reported by the senior Russian PA official in paras 1 and 2 above, including the reasons for Sergei IVANOV's dismissal, was corroborated independently by a former top level Russian intelligence officer and Kremlin insider, also in mid-September.

14 September 2016

24

COMPANY INTELLIGENCE REPORT 2016/112

RUSSIA/US PRESIDENTIAL ELECTION: KREMLIN-ALPHA GROUP CO-OPERATION

Summary

- Top level Russian official confirms current closeness of Alpha Group-PUTIN relationship. Significant favours continue to be done in both directions and FRIDMAN and AVEN still giving informal advice to PUTIN, especially on the US

- Key intermediary in PUTIN-Alpha relationship identified as Oleg GOVORUN, currently Head of a Presidential Administration department but throughout the 1990s, the Alpha executive who delivered illicit cash directly to PUTIN

- PUTIN personally unbothered about Alpha's current lack of investment in Russia but under pressure from colleagues over this and able to exploit it as lever over Alpha interlocutors

Detail

1. Speaking to a trusted compatriot in mid-September 2016, a top level Russian government official commented on the history and current state of relations between President PUTIN and the Alpha Group of businesses led by oligarchs Mikhail FRIDMAN, Petr AVEN and German KHAN. The Russian government figure reported that although they had had their ups and downs, the leading figures in Alpha currently were on very good terms with PUTIN. Significant favours continued to be done in both directions, primarily political ones for PUTIN and business/legal ones for Alpha. Also, FRIDMAN and AVEN continued to give informal advice to PUTIN on foreign policy, and especially about the US where he distrusted advice being given to him by officials.

2. Although FRIDMAN recently had met directly with PUTIN in Russia, much of the dialogue and business between them was mediated through a senior Presidential Administration official, Oleg GOVORUN, who currently headed the department therein responsible for Social Co-operation With the CIS. GOVORUN was trusted by PUTIN and recently had accompanied him to Uzbekistan to pay respects at the tomb of former president KARIMOV. However according to the top level Russian government official, during the 1990s GOVORUN had been Head of Government Relations at Alpha Group and in reality, the "driver" and "bag carrier"

used by FRIDMAN and AVEN to deliver large amounts of illicit cash to the Russian president, at that time deputy Mayor of St Petersburg. Given that and the continuing sensitivity of the PUTIN-Alpha relationship, and need for plausible deniability, much of the contact between them was now indirect and entrusted to the relatively low profile GOVORUN.

3. The top level Russian government official described the PUTIN-Alpha relationship as both carrot and stick. Alpha held 'kompromat' on PUTIN and his corrupt business activities from the 1990s whilst although not personally overly bothered by Alpha's failure to reinvest the proceeds of its TNK oil company sale into the Russian economy since, the Russian president was able to use pressure on this count from senior Kremlin colleagues as a lever on FRIDMAN and AVEN to make them do his political bidding.

14 September 2016

26

COMPANY INTELLIGENCE REPORT 2016/113

RUSSIA/US PRESIDENTIAL ELECTION- REPUBLICAN CANDIDATE TRUMP'S PRIOR ACTIVITIES IN ST PETERSBURG

Summary

- Two knowledgeable St Petersburg sources claim Republican candidate TRUMP has paid bribes and engaged in sexual activities there but key witnesses silenced and evidence hard to obtain

- Both believe Azeri business associate of TRUMP, Araz AGALAROV will know the details

Detail

1. Speaking to a trusted compatriot in September 2016, two well-placed sources based in St Petersburg, one in the political/business elite and the other involved in the local services and tourist industry, commented on Republican US presidential candidate Donald TRUMP's prior activities in the city.

2. Both knew TRUMP had visited St Petersburg on several occasions in the past and had been interested in doing business deals there involving real estate. The local business/political elite figure reported that TRUMP had paid bribes there to further his interests but very discreetly and only through affiliated companies, making it very hard to prove. The local services industry source reported that TRUMP had participated in sex parties in the city too, but that all direct witnesses to this recently had been "silenced" i.e. bribed or coerced to disappear.

3. The two St Petersburg figures cited believed an Azeri business figure, Araz AGALAROV (with offices in Baku and London) had been closely involved with TRUMP in Russia and would know most of the details of what the Republican presidential candidate had got up to there.

14 September 2016

RUSSIA: KREMLIN ASSESSMENT OF TRUMP AND RUSSIAN INTERFERENCE IN US PRESIDENTIAL ELECTION

Summary

- Buyer's remorse sets in with Kremlin over TRUMP support operation in US presidential election. Russian leadership disappointed that leaked e-mails on CLINTON have not had greater impact in campaign

- Russians have injected further anti-CLINTON material into the 'plausibly deniable' leaks pipeline which will continue to surface, but best material already in public domain

- PUTIN angry with senior officials who "overpromised" on TRUMP and further heads likely to roll as result. Foreign Minister LAVROV may be next

- TRUMP supported by Kremlin because seen as divisive, anti-establishment candidate who would shake up current international status quo in Russia's favor. Lead on TRUMP operation moved from Foreign Ministry to FSB and then to presidential administration where it now sits

Detail

1. Speaking separately in confidence to a trusted compatriot in early October 2016, a senior Russian leadership figure and a Foreign Ministry official reported on recent developments concerning the Kremlin's operation to support Republican candidate Donald TRUMP in the US presidential election. The senior leadership figure said that a degree of buyer's remorse was setting in among Russian leaders concerning TRUMP. PUTIN and his colleagues were surprised and disappointed that leaks of Democratic candidate, Hillary CLINTON's hacked e-mails had not had greater impact on the campaign.

2. Continuing on this theme, the senior leadership figure commented that a stream of further hacked CLINTON material already had been injected by the Kremlin into compliant western media outlets like Wikileaks, which remained at least "plausibly deniable", so the stream of these would continue through October and up to the election. However s/he understood that the best material the Russians had already was out and there were no real game-changers to come.

3. The Russian Foreign Ministry official, who had direct access to the TRUMP support operation, reported that PUTIN was angry at his subordinate's "over-promising" on the Republican presidential candidate, both in terms of his chances and reliability and being able to cover and/or contain the US backlash over Kremlin interference. More heads therefore were likely to roll, with the MFA the easiest target. Ironically, despite his consistent urging of caution on the issue, Foreign Minister LAVROV could be the next one to go.

4. Asked to explain why PUTIN and the Kremlin had launched such an aggressive TRUMP support operation in the first place, the MFA official said that Russia needed to upset the liberal international status quo, including on Ukraine-related sanctions, which was seriously

disadvantaging the country. TRUMP was viewed as divisive in disrupting the whole US political system; anti-Establishment; and a pragmatist with whom they could do business. As the TRUMP support operation had gained momentum, control of it had passed from the MFA to the FSB and then into the presidential administration where it remained, a reflection of its growing significance over time. There was still a view in the Kremlin that TRUMP would continue as a (divisive) political force even if he lost the presidency and may run for and be elected to another public office.

12 October 2016

29

RUSSIA/US PRESIDENTIAL ELECTION: FURTHER DETAILS OF KREMLIN LIAISON WITH TRUMP CAMPAIGN

Summary

- Close associate of SECHIN confirms his secret meeting in Moscow with Carter PAGE in July

- Substance included offer of large stake in Rosneft in return for lifting sanctions on Russia. PAGE confirms this is TRUMP's intention

- SECHIN continued to think TRUMP could win presidency up to 17 October. Now looking to reorientate his engagement with the US

- Kremlin insider highlights importance of TRUMP's lawyer, Michael COHEN in covert relationship with Russia. COHEN's wife is of Russian descent and her father a leading property developer in Moscow

Detail

1. Speaking to a trusted compatriot in mid October 2016, a close associate of Rosneft President and PUTIN ally Igor' SECHIN elaborated on the reported secret meeting between the latter and Carter PAGE, of US Republican presidential candidate's foreign policy team, in Moscow in July 2016. The secret meeting had been confirmed to him/her by a senior member of SECHIN's staff, in addition to by the Rosneft President himself. It took place on either 7 or 8 July, the same day or the one after Carter PAGE made a public speech to the Higher Economic School in Moscow.

2. In terms of the substance of their discussion, SECHIN's associate said that the Rosneft President was so keen to lift personal and corporate western sanctions imposed on the company, that he offered PAGE/TRUMP's associates the brokerage of up to a 19 per cent (privatised) stake in Rosneft in return. PAGE had expressed interest and confirmed that were TRUMP elected US president, then sanctions on Russia would be lifted.

3. According to SECHIN's close associate, the Rosneft President had continued to believe that TRUMP could win the US presidency right up to 17 October, when he assessed this was no longer possible. SECHIN was keen to re-adapt accordingly and put feelers out to other business and political contacts in the US instead.

4. Speaking separately to the same compatriot in mid-October 2016, a Kremlin insider with direct access to the leadership confirmed that a key role in the secret TRUMP campaign/Kremlin relationship was being played by the Republican candidate's personal lawyer Michael COHEN ▄▄▄▄▄▄▄▄▄▄▄▄▄▄▄▄▄▄▄▄▄▄▄▄▄▄▄▄▄▄▄▄▄▄▄

30

Source Comment

5. SECHIN's associate opined that although PAGE had not stated it explicitly to SECHIN, he had clearly implied that in terms of his comment on TRUMP's intention to lift Russian sanctions if elected president, he was speaking with the Republican candidate's authority.

Company Comment

6. ███

18 October 2016

COMPANY INTELLIGENCE REPORT 2016/135

RUSSIA/US PRESIDENTIAL ELECTION: THE IMPORTANT ROLE OF TRUMP
LAWYER, COHEN IN CAMPAIGN'S SECRET LIAISON WITH THE KREMLIN

Summary

- Kremlin insider outlines important role played by TRUMP's lawyer
  COHEN in secret liaison with Russian leadership

- COHEN engaged with Russians in trying to cover up scandal of
  MANAFORT and exposure of PAGE and meets Kremlin officials secretly in
  the EU in August in pursuit of this goal

- These secret contacts continue but are now farmed out to trusted agents
  in Kremlin-linked institutes so as to remain "plausibly deniable" for
  Russian regime

- Further confirmation that sacking of IVANOV and appointments of VAINO
  and KIRIYENKO linked to need to cover up Kremlin's TRUMP support
  operation

Detail

1. Speaking in confidence to a longstanding compatriot friend in mid-
   October 2016, a Kremlin insider highlighted the importance of
   Republican presidential candidate Donald TRUMP's lawyer, Michael
   COHEN, in the ongoing secret liaison relationship between the New York
   tycoon's campaign and the Russian leadership. COHEN's role had grown
   following the departure of Paul MANNAFORT as TRUMP's campaign
   manager in August 2016. Prior to that MANNAFORT had led for the
   TRUMP side.

2. According to the Kremlin insider, COHEN now was heavily engaged in a
   cover up and damage limitation operation in the attempt to prevent the
   full details of TRUMP's relationship with Russia being exposed. In
   pursuit of this aim, COHEN had met secretly with several Russian
   Presidential Administration (PA) Legal Department officials in an EU
   country in August 2016. The immediate issues had been to contain
   further scandals involving MANNAFORT's commercial and political role
   in Russia/Ukraine and to limit the damage arising from exposure of
   former TRUMP foreign policy advisor, Carter PAGE's secret meetings
   with Russian leadership figures in Moscow the previous month. The

overall objective had been to "to sweep it all under the carpet and make sure no connections could be fully established or proven"

3. Things had become even "hotter" since August on the TRUMP-Russia track. According to the Kremlin insider, this had meant that direct contact between the TRUMP team and Russia had been farmed out by the Kremlin to trusted agents of influence working in pro-government policy institutes like that of Law and Comparative Jurisprudence. COHEN however continued to lead for the TRUMP team.

4. Referring back to the (surprise) sacking of Sergei IVANOV as Head of PA in August 2016, his replacement by Anton VAINO and the appointment of former Russian premier Sergei KIRIYENKO to another senior position in the PA, the Kremlin insider repeated that this had been directly connected to the TRUMP support operation and the need to cover up now that it was being exposed by the USG and in the western media.

Company Comment

The Kremlin insider was unsure of the identities of the PA officials with whom COHEN met secretly in August, or the exact date/s and locations of the meeting/s. There were significant internal security barriers being erected in the PA as the TRUMP issue became more controversial and damaging. However s/he continued to try to obtain these.

19 October 2016

COMPANY INTELLIGENCE REPORT 2016/166

US/RUSSIA: FURTHER DETAILS OF SECRET DIALOGUE BETWEEN TRUMP CAMPAIGN TEAM, KREMLIN AND ASSOCIATED HACKERS IN PRAGUE

Summary

- TRUMP's representative COHEN accompanied to Prague in August/September 2016 by 3 colleagues for secret discussions with Kremlin representatives and associated operators/hackers

- Agenda included how to process deniable cash payments to operatives; contingency plans for covering up operations; and action in event of a CLINTON election victory

- Some further details of Russian representatives/operatives involved; Romanian hackers employed; and use of Bulgaria as bolt hole to "lie low"

- Anti-CLINTON hackers and other operatives paid by both TRUMP team and Kremlin, but with ultimate loyalty to Head of PA, IVANOV and his successor/s

Detail

1. We reported previously (2016/135 and /136) on secret meeting/s held in Prague, Czech Republic in August 2016 between then Republican presidential candidate Donald TRUMP's representative, Michael COHEN and his interlocutors from the Kremlin working under cover of Russian 'NGO' Rossotrudnichestvo.

2. ██ provided further details of these meeting/s and associated anti-CLINTON/Democratic Party operations. COHEN had been accompanied to Prague by 3 colleagues and the timing of the visit was either in the last week of August or the first week of September. One of their main Russian interlocutors was Oleg SOLODUKHIN operating under Rossotrudnichestvo cover. According to ████████████████, the agenda comprised questions on how deniable cash payments were to be made to hackers who had worked in Europe under Kremlin direction against the CLINTON campaign and various contingencies for covering up these operations and Moscow's secret liaison with the TRUMP team more generally.

24

3.   ████████████ reported that over the period March-September 2016 a company called ████████ and its affiliates had been using botnets and porn traffic to transmit viruses, plant bugs, steal data and conduct "altering operations" against the Democratic Party leadership. Entities linked to one ████████████ were involved and he and another hacking expert, both recruited under duress by the FSB, ████ ████████████ were significant players in this operation. In Prague, COHEN agreed contingency plans for various scenarios to protect the operation, but in particular what was to be done in the event that Hillary CLINTON won the presidency. It was important in this event that all cash payments owed were made quickly and discreetly and that cyber and other operators were stood down/able to go effectively to ground to cover their traces. (We reported earlier that the involvement of political operatives Paul MANAFORT and Carter PAGE in the secret TRUMP-Kremlin liaison had been exposed in the media in the run-up to Prague and that damage limitation of these also was discussed by COHEN with the Kremlin representatives).

4.   In terms of practical measures to be taken, it was agreed by the two sides in Prague to stand down various "Romanian hackers" (presumably based in their homeland or neighbouring eastern Europe) and that other operatives should head for a bolt-hole in Plovdiv, Bulgaria where they should "lay low". On payments, IVANOV's associate said that the operatives involved had been paid by both TRUMP's team and the Kremlin, though their orders and ultimate loyalty lay with IVANOV, as Head of the PA and thus ultimately responsible for the operation, and his designated successor/s after he was dismissed by president PUTIN in connection with the anti-CLINTON operation in mid August.

13 December 2016

Made in the USA
Middletown, DE
18 July 2023

35377952R10022